Wheels, Wheels, Wheels

Helena Ramsay and
Paul Humphrey

Illustrated by

Stuart Trotter

King's Road Primary School
Rosyth - Tel: 313470

6

Small wheels have to go round much
faster than big wheels if they're to move
along the ground at the same speed.

A hundred years ago some bikes had one very big wheel and one small one.

I know, they were called penny farthings.

9

When you change gear the chain moves
from one cog to another.

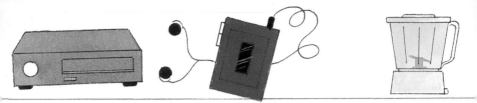

We can see the cog-wheels on a bike but lots of machines have wheels inside them which you can't see.

Some watches have wheels.

Did you know that there are wheels inside a cassette recorder, too? The wheels turn the cassette tape.

Sometimes they used animals
to help them. Otherwise they
pushed or dragged the
things themselves.
It was hard work.

Wheels make it much easier and
faster to move things around.

Here's the building site.
Let's look at all the different
kinds of wheels.

That dumper truck
has got big, fat wheels.

Big, fat wheels don't sink into the ground. The dumper truck can go over soft earth without getting stuck.

There's a bulldozer, it hasn't got any wheels.

A bulldozer has got wheels inside the caterpillar tracks. They make the tracks go round.

Did you know that wheels can be used for lifting things, too?

Do cranes have wheels?

20

Yes, cranes have pulley wheels with cables around them. That's why they can lift such heavy things.

Wow! Look at the crane now.

It's going to lift that huge girder.

21

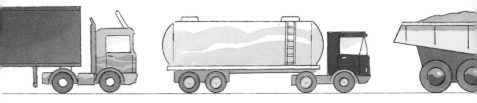

It has lots of wheels so that it can carry very heavy loads. The weight is divided up among all the wheels so that each one carries only a little bit.

23

Here's the funfair at last!

Look at the clown
on that funny bike!

Bikes with only one wheel
are called unicycles.
You have to balance very carefully.

You can all have a ride on the big wheel before we go home.

That's the biggest wheel I've ever seen.

How do they make the big wheel turn round so fast?

There is an engine driving it round.

A motor turns the wheels on my wheelchair.

Look at me making the wheels turn on my skateboard - whoops!

Which is which? Match the wheels to these vehicles:

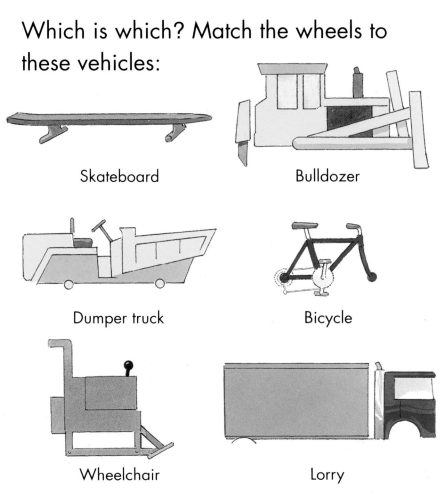

Skateboard

Bulldozer

Dumper truck

Bicycle

Wheelchair

Lorry

The answers are at the bottom of the page, but don't peep until you have tried yourself.